Disney

ALICE IN WONDERLAND

THE VISUAL GUIDE

WRITTEN BY
JO CASEY & LAURA GILBERT

CONTENTS

WELCOME TO UNDERLAND

THERE IS A PLACE like no place on Earth. A land full of wonder, mystery and danger. Some say to survive it you need to be as **mad as a hatter**, which, luckily, I am! Welcome to Underland!

I can guarantee that you will never have seen anywhere as **gallymoggers** as this place I call home. We've got everything here: a garden with Talking Flowers, a forest filled with mushrooms, the red desert of Crims and the muddy bogs of Gummer Slough.

And it's not just strange* places; the strangest things happen in Underland. Not that long ago the sky rained fish for no apparent reason, and when the gracious White Queen ruled over us, we would celebrate **Keltikidik**. This was a day when everyone wore white, drank milk and could only tell white lies.

What a **naughty Hatter!** I'm letting my memory run away from me. Memory... **mmmm**... that reminds me. I've been considering things that begin with the letter "m": moron, mutiny, murder, malice.... Where was I? Ah yes! Underland! It's bizarre, dangerous, absurd, but oh so very beautiful. And if you get a teensy bit hungry, pop round to the March Hare's house for tea. There will be scones and cream and Battenburg cake and tea, and....Aargh! I'm late. The March Hare will be mad as a hatter. Oh no, that's me!

Fairfarren, my new friend. Enjoy your time in Underland. And remember: the impossible is possible. Just look around you.

Tarrant, the Mad Hatter

* "Strange" to you that is. To us Outlanders, this is as normal as can be!

INTRODUCTION

Young Alice Kingsleigh feels that no one understands her and that she doesn't understand others. She has been raised in a world where there are certain rules that everyone must abide by and where "improper" behaviour is frowned upon. What Alice doesn't know yet is that another completely different land exists, a land that is wondrous and fantastical, where rabbits wear waistcoats and flowers can talk... a land called Underland.

However, since the Horunvendush Day, Underland has been a gloomy, scary place to live. This was the day when the cruel Red Queen took control of Underland from her sister, the gentle White Queen. A group has formed that is opposed to the Red Queen called the Underland Underground Resistance. But the only way to free the people of Underland from the Red Queen's terrifying reign is to slay the Red Queen's fearsome Jabberwocky, using the Vorpal Sword. Rumour has it that there is only one person who can do this and save Underland. Her name is Alice Kingsleigh.

Join Alice on the biggest adventure of her life as she learns that anything is possible... and that dreams really do come true.

ALICE

Young Alice loved to play with her dolls and dress up in different costumes and hats. Her favourite hat was a black top hat.

ALICE KINGSLEIGH LIVES with her mother in London. Her father passed away when she was young and Alice has felt slightly out of place ever since. Now she is a young woman, she is trying to discover who she truly is. Never one to toe the line, Alice is confused by everyone telling her what is best for her. If only she could have a moment to work out what it is that *she* wants.

Daddy's Girl
Alice and her father, Charles, were very close. Alice sometimes feels that he was the only person who truly understood her. Charles taught Alice that anything was possible and that all the best people were mad as hatters!

"MY FATHER SAID HE SOMETIMES BELIEVED IN SIX IMPOSSIBLE THINGS BEFORE BREAKFAST."

Points of View
Alice loves her mother, Helen, very much, but she does not enjoy being told what to do by her. Helen prefers to do what is proper, whereas Alice thinks you should only behave in a manner that you believe in.

10

The Thinker

Whether it is standing up for one of her beloved family or being honest when something doesn't make sense to her, Alice is not afraid to speak her mind. She also likes to be able to explain things rationally, but Alice will soon learn that not everything in life has a logical explanation.

Big Dream

Alice wants her independence and she is determined to get it. Everyone expects her to marry into the aristocracy and to stay close to home, but Alice wants more from her life. Maybe one day her dream will come true.

Alice has a curious recurring dream about a smiling cat, a rabbit in a waistcoat and a dodo with a walking cane. Her father tells her that it is only a dream and that dreams cannot harm her.

Alice is against wearing a corset, much to her mother's despair.

Delicate striped gloves add a touch of individuality to Alice's outfit.

Alice's dress is made out of blue silk and elegant lace.

11

ALICE'S FAMILY

EVERYONE IN ALICE'S family has an opinion on what Alice should do with her life, and they seem to have her whole future mapped out for her. But Alice sees the world differently to them. She misses her father, Charles, terribly. If he were here he would know exactly what she should do...

Charles Kingsleigh

Alice could always rely on her father to reassure her if she was having her bad dream. Alice and Charles were very similar and without him, she feels that there is no one like her in the world.

Charles Kingsleigh owned a trading company. His colleagues thought he had lost his senses when he wanted to expand his trading route to Asia. But Charles always believed that "the only way to achieve the impossible is to believe it is possible", a belief he has passed on to his daughter.

Aunt Imogene

Imogene is Alice's spinster aunt. She is waiting for her fiancé, a prince who cannot marry her unless he renounces his throne. It is a truly tragic tale but one that is entirely in Aunt Imogene's imagination. She'll be waiting a long time for her prince to come along...

Helen Kingsleigh

Alice's mother, Helen, has to bring up Alice alone after the death of her husband. She wants what is best for her daughter, but she sometimes struggles with Alice's stubborn and determined nature. She thinks that Alice won't get the best if she doesn't conform – not wearing stockings is not her idea of "proper" behaviour.

"WHO'S TO SAY WHAT IS PROPER?"

Margaret Manchester

Alice's sister, Margaret, believes that she has the perfect marriage with her husband, Lowell, and wants Alice to have the same. She tells Alice that Hamish Ascot, son of Lord and Lady Ascot, wants to marry her and it has all been arranged. After all, Alice can't do much better than a lord and, as Margaret reminds her, her pretty face won't last forever.

Lowell Manchester

Margaret's husband, Lowell, appears to be the perfect gentleman, and Margaret certainly believes so. However, Alice finds him partaking in some decidedly ungentlemanly behaviour – kissing a woman who isn't his wife! That is definitely not what Helen Kingsleigh would call "proper" behaviour.

ALICE'S ACQUAINTANCES

THE KINGSLEIGHS HAVE friends in high places. The noble Lord and Lady Ascot are even holding a summer party in Alice's honour – or that is what Alice thinks. Actually, it is really a secret engagement party for Hamish and an unsuspecting Alice. But with the Chattaway sisters around, it won't be a secret for long!

Summer Party

Lord and Lady Ascot expect punctuality in all their guests. They have laid on a spectacular summer party with croquet, a string quartet and dancing. Only the best will do for their beloved son, Hamish.

Lord Ascot

Lord Ascot has bought Charles Kingsleigh's company. He was Charles' good friend and his only regret is that he didn't invest in Charles' venture to expand the business when Charles was alive.

Lady Ascot

Lady Ascot has been planning this engagement party for the last 20 years and anything less than perfect simply will not do. Her greatest fear in life is having ugly grandchildren, but she is sure that with Alice's good looks this won't happen.

Dancing

Alice finds dancing a quadrille with a strutting Hamish a bore. She would much rather imagine what it would be like to fly, but pompous Hamish thinks this is best kept to herself.

Alice and Hamish aren't the perfect match that everyone wants them to be. Alice has a vivid imagination, whereas practical Hamish believes daydreaming is an utter waste of time.

"AT LAST! WE THOUGHT YOU'D NEVER ARRIVE."

The Chattaways

Giggly and gossipy, Faith and Fiona Chattaway find it tough to keep a secret. They chat away so much that they can't help but let on to Alice that Hamish is going to propose to her!

In the gardens, Alice thinks she sees a rabbit dart past. Lady Ascot hates rabbits! This combined with the fact that her gardeners have planted the wrong colour roses leaves Lady Ascot annoyed. However, she manages to calm down enough to tell Alice that Hamish has a delicate digestion. Alice couldn't be less interested.

EAT ME, DRINK ME

WHEN ALICE SPIES a White Rabbit wearing a waistcoat, she wonders whether it is her turn to start believing in the impossible. Regardless, Alice thinks that a giant rabbit is far more interesting than a dull garden party and swiftly follows the bounding bunny.

Heading for a Fall

Alice loses sight of the White Rabbit until a paw grabs her and pulls her down a hole. As she plummets past crystal balls and human skulls, Alice thinks it odd that she thought her life was out of control before!

Sweet Dreams

Alice is used to bizarre dreams, but this is the oddest one yet! She keeps telling herself it is just a dream and considers pinching herself to wake up, but nothing works. Things are still very weird.

Alice's pretty dress wasn't made for tumbling down muddy rabbit holes.

16

Closed Doors

Alice finds herself in a Round Hall with lots of little doors. Each one is locked but there is a tiny key on top of a glass table. Alice tries the key in each door and finally finds the correct fit. Through the open door, Alice sees a beautiful – and strange – garden.

A lice is a well-mannered young woman, who learned the art of etiquette from her parents. When a bottle of liquid, labelled with the words "Drink Me", appears on the table, polite Alice does as she's told. It tastes vile, but the drink has a remarkable shrinking effect on Alice and she becomes small enough to fit through the door. However, the door is now locked and the key is atop the towering table!

This miniature cake, iced with the words "Eat Me", looks harmless, but Alice thought the same about the bottle of liquid!

All Grown Up

One bite of the cake and Alice shoots up, as quickly as she shrank. Thinking on her giant feet, she unlocks the door. She then drinks from the bottle to shrink herself and walks through the door. Alice hopes she won't have to go through any more ups and downs.

ROUND AND ROUND

The vast Round Hall at the end of the long rabbit hole is certainly mysterious. The many doors are all different shapes and sizes, much like everything else is in Underland, and no one has any idea whether they all lead to the same place.

"It's only a DREAM."

WHITE RABBIT

THE WHITE RABBIT, McTwisp, is forever hopping hither and thither. After all, there are Alices to find and trumpets to blow. Stylish, squeamish and ever-punctual, court page McTwisp never leaves home without his pocket watch... and a suitably dapper waistcoat.

Anxious McTwisp is never late – he doesn't want to upset Time!

On the Hop

The White Rabbit can always be relied upon to do a job properly. He is chosen to go up into the real world and find the "real" Alice. It is no easy task – McTwisp almost gets eaten by other animals, and the least he expects is some gratitude!

"I TOLD YOU SHE'S THE RIGHT ALICE."

20

The Rabbit Hole

McTwisp has been searching high and low for the right Alice so he can lead her to the rabbit hole and down into Underland. Luckily for McTwisp, once he has found Alice, it doesn't take long for her curiosity to get the better of her. She runs after the White Rabbit, peers into the hole and promptly falls down it!

Alice's journey down the rabbit hole is a hair-raising one! The rabbit hole is full of the strange things that McTwisp hoards there, including cracked mirrors, demonic masks and a monkey's hand.

As well as his watch, the White Rabbit also carries a trumpet. He sounds it at state events to announce arrivals or even to declare the start of a battle, though fretful McTwisp isn't particularly fond of these occasions.

Gold-plated trumpet.

Court Page

Quick, efficient and organized, McTwisp makes an excellent court page. He served in the White Queen's court as her personal page and enjoyed the level of responsibility – and the pristine uniform.

21

WONDERFUL UNDERLAND
Taking her first steps into Underland, Alice finds herself surrounded by massive mushrooms and giant Talking Flowers that have human faces. It is a strange and beautiful land – and only the beginning of Alice's wonderful adventure.

"LITTLE IMPOSTER!
PRETENDING TO BE ALICE!"

DORMOUSE

MALLYMKUN MAY BE a dormouse but she is certainly not mousy! This feisty creature is determined, brave and always *en garde*. When she is not taking tea with the Mad Hatter and the March Hare, she is busy sharpening her hat pin, donning her breeches and preparing for the next battle.

Daring Dormouse
Mallymkun is brave and defiant. Whether it is fighting a beast like the Bandersnatch or contemplating how to escape her imprisonment by the Red Queen's Knave, the Dormouse refuses to give in. Utterly fearless, Mallymkun will never beg for mercy.

"I DON'T TAKE ORDERS..."

Partners in Crime
Mallymkun is the Mad Hatter's sidekick. She brings him back to reality when he gets crazy. The Hatter considers Mallymkun to be just a close friend, but she is secretly in love with the Hatter.

The Dormouse's weapon of choice is a hat pin, given to her by the Mad Hatter. Like Mallymkun, it may only be small but it is deadly! It is also highly versatile. The Dormouse uses it to wake people from dreams, poke eyes and pick locks.

This sharp hat pin could take someone's eye out – and it has!

The Dormouse keeps the Bandersnatch's eye tied to her belt.

Bull's-eye

There is nothing meek about this mouse! The Dormouse's battle with the Red Queen's beast, the Bandersnatch, is her greatest to date. As soon as she saw Alice in trouble, she pounced on the Bandersnatch and stabbed him in the eye with her hat pin. Now Mallymkun wears the eye as a trophy – and a warning to others who dare to cross her path.

Mallymkun reluctantly wears the Red Queen's colours.

The Bandersnatch met its match in the Dormouse. What Mallymkun lacks in size, she more than makes up for with sharp sword skills.

TWEEDLEDUM AND TWEEDLEDEE

IT IS VIRTUALLY impossible to tell Tweedledum and Tweedledee apart. However, this contrary pair might look alike and speak alike but that doesn't mean that they think alike – if Dum says "east to Queast" you can be sure that Dee will say "south to Snud".

Caught in the Middle

The bickering Tweedledum and Tweedledee both want to escort Alice to the Caterpillar, Absolem. It's simply not fair if one gets to do it and the other does not. According to the White Rabbit, their contrariness is a family trait, but the Tweedles are sure to disagree with him on this point!

Extra large trousers for extra large waist.

"CONTRARIWISE, I BELIEVE IT SO..."

The perfect canvas for the Red Queen's paints and powders.

Snatched!

Tweedledum and Tweedledee are snatched by the Red Queen's screeching Jubjub bird, a part monkey-eating eagle and part ostrich, and taken to the Red Queen's castle in Salazen Grum. If they thought the Jubjub bird was scary, wait until they meet the Red Queen!

Team Tweedle

When they are not talking in opposites Dee and Dum are pinching and poking each other. In fact, the only time these two aren't bickering is when they are called into battle. They make a surprisingly good team and fight in perfect unison.

Fatboys

The Red Queen thinks that Tweedledee and Tweedledum, or her "Fatboys", are hilarious. She paints red hearts on their faces and orders them to speak. Still, it could be worse – she could have ordered their heads to be chopped off!

The Tweedles are in agreement that black and white stripes suit them.

CATERPILLAR

ABSOLEM IS THE WISEST being in Underland. Everyone trusts this blue caterpillar and they turn to him for his insightful advice. So, who better to be the keeper of the legendary Oraculum? He is also the perfect one to explain to Alice her destiny: she is the person who must kill the evil Jabberwocky with the Vorpal Sword, as written in the Oraculum.

Big Thinker

Most individuals who meet the Caterpillar think he is very serious, but he has been known to collapse in heaps of giggles when tickled. At other times, this caterpillar can be found contemplating his own mortality. Absolem knows that he is coming to the end of this life, but that a new life awaits him as a beautiful blue butterfly.

Mushrooms come in many different colours and sizes.

Perfect Perch

Any philosopher needs a restful place to contemplate. Absolem can usually be found sitting atop a mushroom, be it one in the Mushroom Forest or the White Queen's topiary mushroom.

"NOTHING WAS EVER ACCOMPLISHED WITH TEARS."

The Oraculum

The Oraculum is an ancient parchment that tells about every day since the beginning of time. This astonishing document shows what has happened, what will happen and what is currently happening. Absolem guards the parchment with great care.

ORACULUM

IMAGINE A COMPENDIUM that could reveal the past, present and future of Underland. The Oraculum does exactly that. This ancient parchment scroll chronicles the major events of each and every day since the Beginning. Each event is depicted by a beautiful illustration.

The fearsome Jabberwocky before he shoots fire at the Hightopp Clan of Underland on the Horunvendush Day.

Hightopp hat.

The March Hare enjoying a soothing cup of tea.

The Hightopp Clan go around the Maypole on the Horunvendush Day.

Not-so-ordinary Oraculum

The Oraculum's black and white detailed illustrations depict each and every day. At first glance it might look ordinary, but when the Oraculum is opened each illustration comes to life!

Alice's Fate

Alice sees her future right before her very eyes when the Caterpillar shows her the Frabjous Day in the Oraculum. This is the day that Alice will slay the Jabberwocky. The illustration clearly shows a knight with long blonde hair victoriously standing atop a slain Jabberwocky!

"IT LOOKS SO ORDINARY FOR AN ORACLE."

Absolem shows Alice the Griblig Day in the Oraculum. The illustration shows the Tweedles, the March Hare, Alice and the Dodo looking at the Oraculum at the exact same moment!

The Mad Hatter at the Tea Party that has been going on for years.

The Dormouse holding on to her super-sharp hatpin.

In Underland, teatime is all the time!

BANDERSNATCH

IT IS FAIR to say that the Red Queen has a lot of enemies. That's why she keeps a vicious guard dog. The Bandersnatch is a huge, horrifying creature that strikes terror in all who live in Underland. With its thunderous roar and razor-sharp teeth, it is a terrifying sight to behold – just not to a tiny Dormouse...

Big Barrier

Everything about the Bandersnatch is big and strong! The Bandersnatch's smell is so potent, it is enough to knock anyone out within breathing distance, while its huge roar can scare a person witless. If Alice survives all that, there is always the danger that the Bandersnatch may eat her for breakfast!

The mesh net keeps the eyeball secure.

Alice needs the Vorpal Sword in order to slay the Jabberwocky. Unfortunately, the key to the box that houses the sword hangs around the Bandersnatch's neck!

When the Bandersnatch tries to attack Alice, the Dormouse bravely rescues her by stabbing the beast in the eye with her hat pin. As the Dormouse pulls the hat pin out, the Bandersnatch's whole eye pops out, too! She is so pleased that she wears it as a souvenir on her breeches.

On Guard

The Bandersnatch prevents trespassers from entering the Red Queen's castle. It might be furry, but it is definitely not cuddly – one look at this ugly beast is usually enough to scare off any unwanted visitors.

Shark-like teeth stained with blood.

Big Softy

Despite the Dormouse's attempts to save Alice, the Bandersnatch lashes out at Alice with its razor-sharp claws. Amazingly, when Alice later returns the eyeball to the Bandersnatch, it changes from vicious beast to gentle giant and licks her wound clean. Maybe its bark is worse than its bite!

JABBERWOCKY

THIS TERRIFYING CREATURE is the Red Queen's darling Jabberwocky and her ultimate weapon. She has used this brutal beast to destroy the Mad Hatter's family – the Hightopp Clan – and the people of Underland live in fear of this vicious creature. The Jabberwocky can only be slain with the Vorpal Sword, but few dare to get near this fanged, fearsome being.

The Vorpal Sword is locked in an ornately engraved box and is guarded by the Bandersnatch.

Frabjous Day

Alice doesn't believe the Caterpillar when he shows her the Oraculum and says that she is the one to kill the Jabberwocky with the Vorpal Sword on the Frabjous Day. When the Mad Hatter also tells Alice a tale from the Outlands that describes her defeat of the beast, she begins to worry.

Ancient Enemy

The Vorpal Sword is the only weapon that can kill the Jabberwocky and it must be wielded by the correct individual. The sword is beautifully crafted: its hilt is adorned with blue jewels and its blade is studded with pale stones. The sword is exceedingly sharp, but cannot be used for any purpose other than to slay the Jabberwocky.

34

Fearful Beast

The Red Queen's "Jabberbabywocky" is nowhere near as helpless as a baby. One whip of the Jabberwocky's sharply pronged tail can fell a bystander, while its ability to shoot fire leaves its foes burned to a crisp. The brutal beast eclipses all others as it swoops down on its prey, with its eyes aflame and its long sharp claws at the ready.

The Jabberwocky is not simply a senseless slayer. Surprisingly, this frightening beast can speak, and very eloquently at that. Alice is shocked, though she should be used to talking creatures by now – Underland is full of them!

"SO MY OLD FOE, WE MEET ON THE BATTLEFIELD ONCE AGAIN."

CREEPY CROSSROADS

The gardens of Underland are a world away from the beautifully manicured grounds of Lord and Lady Ascot's estate. Underland is wild, overgrown, slightly eerie – and so much more exciting than the perfectly neat and terribly proper gardens of London.

"EAST TO **QUEAST**... SOUTH TO **SNUD**."

RED QUEEN

IRACEBETH, THE RED QUEEN OF CRIMS, wasn't always heartless. Her sister, the White Queen, remembers a time when she even got along with her sister, 'Racie, but things are different now. The Red Queen's study of Dominion Over Living Things has made her a feared leader, and her frequent cry of "Off with his head" means her scared subjects obey her every command.

Bighead

The most striking thing about the Red Queen is the size of her head – it is huge! Alice thinks it is bloated and the White Queen thinks it is a growth, but neither would say so to Iracebeth. The Red Queen is so obsessed that she has a mirror that makes her humongous head look smaller and a room of hats to cover her gigantic globe!

Heart to Heart

The Red Queen only has eyes for the Knave of Hearts. The feeling is not mutual, but the Red Queen knows they will be together one day.

While the Red Queen rules from her ornate throne, she is attended by frog footmen and a fish butler.

"IT IS FAR BETTER TO BE FEARED THAN LOVED."

A tiny crown perches on top of the Red Queen's huge head.

For the Chop

Whether it is a frog footman who has stolen her squimberry tarts or someone who flirts with the Knave, the Red Queen's response is always the same – off with their heads! This ruthless ruler is fixated with heads!

Iracebeth wields an ornamental sceptre.

Iracebeth rarely sees things favourably, even through these rose-coloured spectacles. Mostly she sees red.

Red Rule

The Red Queen is not a popular monarch. She removed her sister from the throne and unleashed the Jabberwocky on the Hightopp Clan, leaving the Mad Hatter as the only survivor. The Underland Underground Resistance exists to overthrow Iracebeth: Downal wyth Bluddy Behg Hid!

RED QUEEN'S COURT

To BECOME A courtier to the Red Queen only one crucial criteria has to be met – no inflated egos, just inflated body parts. However, there is only room for one big head at court and that is the Red Queen's! Life at court is very competitive and extremely tiring. It is the courtier's job to praise and flatter the Red Queen at all times because there is always the danger that she may utter those infamous words of hers at any moment...

Court Rules

All of the Red Queen's courtiers are required to have extra-large features. It is also a rule that their faces are painted and powdered, so that they are in keeping with the Red Queen's preferred style.

Lady Long Ears

Lady Long Ears is the Red Queen's eyes and (big) ears around court. She soon has a long face when large Alice arrives and the Red Queen declares that she is her new favourite. So when Lady Long Ears finds out that the Knave of Hearts has a soft spot for Alice, she makes sure that the Red Queen knows all about it.

Red Knights

The Red Queen is not a popular monarch and she has many enemies. Her knights in red armour are always standing guard around court, ready to take orders and defend their queen.

The Red Knights are never without their sharp spears. They use them against any intruders who enter the Red Queen's court unannounced. Don't be fooled by the heart-shaped tips. These spears are definitely not used with love.

Knave of Hearts

The Red Queen wants to be feared by all who know her, except one – her Knave, Ilosovic Stayne. Unfortunately for the Red Queen, Stayne is not in love with her. In fact, she makes him shudder. He would much rather die than spend the rest of his life with her. Stayne is tasked with finding Alice and bringing her to the Red Queen, unharmed. Iracebeth wants to have the pleasure of beheading Alice herself.

The violent Knave of Hearts is not one to choose his battles carefully. Any opportunity to unsheathe his sword is seized upon by the Knave with relish. However, he likes his victims to put up a bit of a fight. Where's the fun in battle if there is no weeping or begging? Those are the best bits!

This big-bellied courtier is very proud of his protruding belly. However, it is actually fake and is held in place by straps. He would much rather carry extra weight around his middle to please the Red Queen than lose the weight of his head.

RED QUEEN'S CASTLE

The Red Queen's crest displayed on the flags is a heart in flames.

SITTING ON THE TEMPESTUOUS shore of the Crimson sea in Salazen Grum is a dark and menacing sight. Welcome to the Red Queen's castle, where the Red Queen rules over her kingdom. Enter at your peril, for it is not a place for the fainthearted. You have been warned...

Grizzly Welcome

There's only one way to get to the castle doors and that is across a grim moat, which is filled with a red liquid that looks strangely like blood. Stepping stones in the form of heads of the Red Queen's unlucky visitors are kindly provided to get across. The Red Queen certainly doesn't make it easy for her guests!

High walls to keep intruders out.

The Throne Room is where the Red Queen makes all her important decisions, which more often than not involve the words "Head" and "Off with"!

Grim moat is definitely not for swimming in!

"I AM NOT A PATIENT MONARCH!"

Doom and Gloom

The Red Queen's castle has dozens of dungeons to keep her prisoners in. For smaller ones, like the Dormouse, a birdcage prison is available. The dreary dungeons are totally bare. The Red Queen won't even stretch to a chair. No wonder the Mad Hatter looks glum!

Prisoners are kept in this tower.

Animal Cruelty

The Red Queen's monkeys are well-trained and they work hard for their peanuts, holding up tables and chairs, as do the flamingos. She often forgets to feed her frog footmen, but they'd better not steal her tarts – her favourite foods are tadpoles on toast and caviar!

43

COURTLY CROQUET

ORDERING HEADS TO be chopped off every minute of every day can be exhausting! So, the Red Queen likes nothing more than taking some time out from her busy schedule to partake in a leisurely game of croquet.

Don't be fooled by this heart-shaped entrance – the Red Queen is heartless.

The Red Knights stand guard, spears in hand.

Cruel Contest

The Red Queen's croquet game is very different from the traditional game. Look closely at this sad sight: miserable flamingos are used as mallets and unfortunate hedgehogs are tied into balls. The Red Queen is much amused!

Flamingos hold up the arches.

The Red Queen's odd-looking
minions look on.

The Red Queen likes to
show off in front of
her staff.

Croquet is the Red
Queen's favourite sport.

The chance to get some fresh air from
the dark and dingy castle is a relief to
the Red Queen's court. The Red Queen is
no croquet champion however, and she
completely misses the hoop! But her staff
like their heads attached to their necks so
they keep quiet. She is not a team player,
so they won't get the chance to swing a
mallet. Only queens are allowed to play
– that way, there can be only one winner!

45

MAD HATTER

TARRANT IS BEST-KNOWN in Underland for being a milliner – and for being mad! Born in Witzend, he comes from the Hightopp Clan, identifiable by their top hats. The Mad Hatter is quick to reassure people he is "absolutely fine", but the fact that he is on the edge of hysteria suggests otherwise. Although, as Alice says, all the best people are bonkers!

"HAVE I GONE MAD?"

Melancholy Milliner
The Hatter used to be the life and soul of the party (tea or otherwise), but now he is more often mad than happy. However, when the White Queen rules once more, the Hatter has promised he will Futterwacken like never before.

Method in his Madness
Tarrant's descent into madness can be traced back to the Horunvendush Day when the Red Queen set her Jabberwocky on the Hightopp Clan. The Hatter was the only survivor and his feelings of guilt and rage drove him over the edge.

Friends Indeed
The Mad Hatter is the only one who believes that Alice is the Alice who visited Underland before. The pair care for each other, but they will never be compatible: Alice is always too tall or too small!

Tarrant's top hat has plenty of hat pins stuck in it.

Heads Up!

The Dormouse has kept the Hatter calm when he has lost his head, and he wants to return the favour – before she loses hers. Tarrant nobly defends Mallymkun, when the Red Queen picks the pair out for execution.

The Hatter's bright green eyes always look slightly crazed.

Top Hatter

Whether it is a bonnet, a cloche or a boater you are after, the Mad Hatter is head and shoulders above the rest. Tarrant feels best when he is hatting. He has worked for both the White Queen and the Red Queen and on heads large and small.

A DREAM COME TRUE

All the dreams that Alice had of talking dodos and grinning cats were never as vivid as this one. Strange landscapes, fantastical castles and bizarre creatures were to be expected; the chance to make friends that she will never forget was not.

"I'LL MISS YOU WHEN I WAKE UP."

COURT HATTER

EVERY COURT NEEDS a hatter and when it comes to making hats, the Mad Hatter is the best in all of Underland. No head is too big or too small for his marvellous millinery. There is no doubt that his creations are fit for a queen!

Special millinery tools are used to make pretty silk flowers to adorn the hats.

Fancy hat pin.

Sad Hat

The Mad Hatter's family, the Hightopp Clan, has always been employed at court – but all that remains of his clan is this burned and trampled top hat. Without this hat on his head, the Mad Hatter feels completely and utterly lost.

Hatter's Hightopp Clan number.

Bright silk material adds colour and hides some of the burns.

Hatter Originals

With his hat stretcher in hand, the Hatter gets hatting and sets about making fabulous and fantastic creations for the Red Queen's humongous head.

Everyone knows that the Red Queen is prone to dramatics. The finishing touch of a porcupine quill matches her personality perfectly.

The Hatter is nothing if not visionary. He knows that leaves aren't just for trees – they make fabulous decorations too!

The Hatter knows what suits his clients best and he has noticed the Red Queen's penchant for the colour red.

Black and white has always been a classic combination. The Hatter adds some pink netting to this hat to please the Red Queen. Well, pink is almost red!

"THE ABSOLUTE BEST WAY TO TRAVEL IS BY HAT."

It takes more than skill and talent to construct a hat and no hatter would be without all the tools of the trade. The Hatter keeps his trusty chalk, thimble and needles in beautifully decorated, ornate cases. To cut some of the finest silks in the world a blunt pair of scissors just will not do – they must be super-sharp. But it's best not to upset the Hatter when he has these to hand – he has been known to cut all his hard work to shreds in a mad frenzy!

Silver thimble, needles and small scissors.

Silver case is engraved with flowers.

The Hatter is lost without his scissors.

51

CHESHIRE CAT

THE CHESHIRE CAT doesn't need nine lives – he is perfectly happy with the one he's got! Serene Chessur can often be found lounging around and grinning away. That is if you can see him, as Chess can make himself disappear at will. Unlike his friends, Chessur is not part of the Underland Underground Resistance; this laid-back feline prefers not to get involved in politics.

Now You See Him

Chessur is the cat's pyjamas. He can appear as a disembodied head, as a complete cat or disappear entirely. This remarkable talent certainly comes in useful when he has to make a quick getaway.

The Cat and the Hat

The Mad Hatter and the Cheshire Cat have a tricky relationship. When the Hightopp Clan was killed by the Jabberwocky, Chessur disappeared from the scene, fearing for his life. The Hatter blames Chess for what happened that day, but he hopes to win back the Hatter's trust.

Chessur's mesmerizing eyes are the last thing to disappear.

A true Cheshire Cat grin.

Suave Feline

The Cheshire Cat is a dapper tabby. He is eloquently spoken, always smiles and is gentlemanly to Alice. When Alice was injured by the Bandersnatch, Chessur was there to tie her bloody wound with his handkerchief. He even kept the cat in the bag about his disgust of blood to help his new pal.

"ALL THIS TALK OF BLOOD AND SLAYING HAS PUT ME OFF MY TEA."

Courage of a Lion

Chessur has learned his lesson. He wants to show that he can be brave and offers to be the one to slay the Jabberwocky. This fearless feline also takes the place of the Hatter when he is headed for the guillotine. After all, you can't chop off a head that has no body!

53

MARCH HARE

THACKERY, THE MARCH HARE, is a jumpy creature who spends a lot of his time scared! Born in Witzend, the March Hare was a member of the White Queen's court. Now he is the host of Underland's longest Tea Party, which has been going on for years. Even so, people still arrive late for tea, which does little for Thackery's anxiety issues.

Home Sweet Home

It is easy to spot Thackery's house – it looks just like him. The house is thatched with fur, the front looks like a hare's face (with windows like eyes) and the windmill sails resemble large ears! Like the March Hare, the house is wary of new people and has been known to tap Thackery on the head when a stranger comes to visit.

"YOU'RE ALL LATE FOR TEA!"

Head Chef

Thackery is an excellent chef. Afternoon (or all-day) tea is his speciality, but he also makes tasty soup.

The March Hare's Tea Party is the longest in Underland history. The tablecloths are threadbare, the ceramic plates and teapots are chipped with age and the guest list has barely changed. If Thackery had known the party would last this long, he would never have started it!

Mad as a March Hare

The March Hare is happiest sipping a cup of sweet tea and he hates anything that may spoil this enjoyment. When he has been slaving over a hot stove, the least he expects is for his guests to be on time. If they are not, they had better watch out for flying teapots and pepper mills – the March Hare goes hopping mad with latecomers!

Thackery always has a cup of tea in his paw.

55

TEA PARTY

Alice is invited to the Tea Party to meet the Mad Hatter, the March Hare and the Dormouse. When the Mad Hatter tried to kill Time at the Tea Party while waiting for Alice's return, Time took offence and stood still! So, after years of waiting, the gathering has lost its party atmosphere, but the return of Alice soon stirs things up.

Tea Time

The table napkins may be stained and the crockery chipped, but there is still lots of wonderful food on offer at the Tea Party. Sandwiches, cakes, biscuits, raspberry jam and, of course, plenty of tea are sure to keep even the fussiest of guests happy!

Tea is known for its soothing and calming qualities, but years of drinking the stuff doesn't seem to have done much for the March Hare's nerves!

Handpainted teapot.

Tiny Alice

The Knave of Hearts gate-crashes the Tea Party, looking for Alice. The Mad Hatter quickly forces Alice to drink the shrinking juice Pishalver and stuffs Alice into a teapot. The Knave would never think to look there!

"You're ABSOLUTELY ALICE! I'D KNOW YOU ANYWHERE."

Mad Trio

While Alice is hiding in the teapot, the Mad Hatter, the Dormouse and the March Hare attempt to put the Knave of Hearts off her scent by singing silly songs. This seems to confirm to the Knave that they are all mad!

After drinking Pishalver, Alice shrinks to just 15 centimetres.

WHITE QUEEN

Just one look from Mirana's pretty eyes is all it takes to get what she wants. Even the Red Queen's unusual furniture isn't safe from her powerful beauty!

MIRANA, THE WHITE QUEEN, is everything that her sister, the Red Queen, is not: beautiful, gentle and kind. Mirana is adored by the people of Underland. They would risk their lives in order for her to rule again, if only to be safe in the knowledge that they won't lose their heads!

Rivals

Alice has always got on with her sister, Margaret; Mirana has not been so lucky. The White Queen's beauty turns the Red Queen green with envy. Mirana just wants her crown back. All she needs is a champion to step forth and slay the Jabberwocky. If only she could find one....

Mirana is not just a pretty face. Her mother taught her how to concoct medicinal cures and transformational potions. She prepares Pishalver, a shrinking juice, for Alice by mixing together gruesome things, including buttered fingers, a pinch of worm fat and White Queen's spit.

Despite having a jar full of spare eyeballs, Mirana still needs her spyglass to keep a lookout on all the comings and goings at her castle.

Loyal Friend

Bayard the bloodhound is forever faithful to the White Queen and her cause, even when he is otherwise tied up. His family is behind bars at the Red Queen's castle – if he finds Alice he will earn their freedom. But like the loyal friend he is, he leads Alice to the White Queen, Vorpal Sword in her hand.

Shiny white curls.

Unlike her sister, the White Queen adores animals.

"WE DON'T HAVE TO FIGHT."

Healing Power

Mirana's power is in the healing arts and it would go against her vows to bring harm to any living thing. So all creatures great and small would be safe under her rule, with the exception of a few ugly bugs!

WHITE QUEEN'S CASTLE

SITTING HIGH ON a hilltop overlooking the magnificent kingdom of Marmoreal is the dazzling White Queen's castle. A winding path leads up to the imposing castle with its domed turrets and stained glass windows, which let in lots of light. It is warm and welcoming – much like the White Queen herself.

Checkmate

The White Queen's castle is made entirely out of white marble. The White Queen has chosen a "chess" theme: giant chess pieces sit atop huge boulders, and even the lawn is mown to look just like a chessboard.

The long drive allows visitors to marvel at the stunning castle.

On the boil

Mirana has a huge kitchen where she concocts her potions. The March Hare is Mirana's cook so, unless guests want to wear their supper, they should arrive on time!

"WELCOME TO MARMOREAL."

With its many turrets and spires, the White Queen's castle looks daunting, but there are many wonderful things to see. A keen animal lover, Mirana has a topiary garden filled with trees and shrubs shaped into animals, including a giraffe and a flamingo. If her trees ever look sad, she has her staff talk to them in a kindly manner to cheer them up. In the Throne Room is the White Knight's armour. It has been here since Shatterky, the day the White Queen was banished to Marmoreal. It just needs the Vorpal Sword to be brought home to complete it.

Chess pieces are carved into the castle.

All animals welcome.

There's no danger of finding chopped off heads in this serene lake.

Pristine chequered lawn.

UNDERLAND

WHEN ALICE FIRST STEPPED through that small door she entered a land where time can stand still, animals can talk and adventures are always waiting to happen. Underland is unique – no wonder Alice thinks she is dreaming.

The Round Hall

Alice's journey into Underland has a bizarre beginning. After falling into the Round Hall, Alice sees lots of ornate locked doors and one little door behind a curtain, but there is only one key.

Talking Flowers

It is not only the creatures that can talk in Underland. The flowers have human faces and like nothing more than a good gossip. The Talking Flowers grow in a garden that is home to a green pig and enormous gnats.

The Tulgey Wood

The Tulgey Wood is a dark and barren place. Visiting the Tulgey Wood always brings back sad memories for the Mad Hatter. It was here that his clan perished on Horunvendush Day.

Strange Beauty

Underland might look beautiful, but sometimes even beauty has a dark side. The White Queen's garden, with its topiary animals, is probably one of the safest spots to be in.

The Mushroom Forest

There are many different forests in Underland. Perhaps the strangest is the Mushroom Forest, where the mushrooms grow as tall as the trees. Absolem the Caterpillar can often be found sitting atop one of the mushrooms here.

O FRABJOUS DAY

THE RED QUEEN'S SUBJECTS have been waiting a long while for Alice to return to Underland and for the Frabjous Day to dawn – the day when Alice will slay the Jabberwocky. Then the White Queen will rule again and everyone will Futterwacken! The Mad Hatter is the only one who believes that this Alice is the true Alice. Now it is up to Alice to prove him right.

Alice dons the armour of the White Knight, including a large silver shield.

Alice Awakes
Even though it is written in the Oraculum that Alice must slay the Jabberwocky, the White Queen tells Alice that the choice is hers. She finds it all a bit overwhelming and seeks advice from Absolem. Alice begins to remember that her dream of Wonderland, as she called it, was not a dream – she has been here before. She is Alice At Last!

The Vorpal Sword has a mind of its own. All Alice has to do is hold on tight!

Battle Ruins

The battle ruins in Tulgey Wood are the perfect place for a combat of epic proportions. They are brimming with the history of all the previous battles of Underland. The ancient remains afford ample opportunities for Alice to conceal herself from the fearsome Jabberwocky.

The White Queen doesn't want to battle with her sister, but Iracebeth has other ideas. Like a spoiled child, the Red Queen won't surrender her crown without a fight.

Let Battle Commence

Alice cannot believe that she will be able to slay the Jabberwocky. While the pair fight, Alice remembers other things in Underland that she would have thought were impossible. With a newfound confidence, Alice cuts off the Jabberwocky's head using the Vorpal Sword. The reign of Bluddy Behg Hid is finally at an end and the White Queen banishes her sister and the Knave to the Outlands forever. Callou, callay!

NEW ADVENTURES

ALICE HAS HAD the most amazing adventure in Underland but she must say goodbye to her new companions and return to the real world. After all, there are important things she must tell her family and friends. Alice's adventure has transformed her into a confident young woman, ready to take on the world and stand up for what she wants.

Real World

Alice chooses to drink a drop of the Jabberwocky's blood, which allows her to return to the real world. She wakes up back in the real world, dangling from a rabbit hole. Her dress is torn and filthy, and her hair is dishevelled, all of which confuses Alice. What could she have been doing? She thinks she may have fallen and bumped her head. All memory of her adventure in Underland has completely vanished.

Alice Returns

When Alice returns to the party, the guests are shocked by her appearance. But Alice doesn't care what she looks like or about her improper behaviour. She even dances a Futterwacken in front of the guests!

Ambitious Alice

Alice has a proposal for Lord Ascot. She thinks that his company should be the first to trade with China. Lord Ascot sees that Alice has inherited her father's vision and ambition. He is so impressed with Alice's confidence, he offers her an apprenticeship with the company. Her father would have been proud.

Alice is now an assured young woman who knows exactly what she believes in. She tells Hamish that she cannot marry him, lets Lady Ascot know that, unlike her, she *loves* rabbits and makes sure Lowell realizes she will be watching him very closely. While dispensing her frank words, Alice can't help noticing the Chattaways' resemblance to some funny boys she met in a dream...

"I'LL FIND SOMETHING USEFUL TO DO WITH MY LIFE."

New Horizons

Alice has said goodbye to her friends and family and is ready to set sail into her future with Lord Ascot's company in China. Before she leaves, a beautiful blue butterfly lands on her shoulder. Alice recognizes Absolem in his new form, come to say goodbye. Maybe Alice hasn't forgotten her new friends after all.

Alice's mother and sister, and also Lord Ascot, gather to bid farewell to Alice as she embarks on her new adventure.

GLOSSARY

OUTLANDISH

Bandersnatch, the: *A ferocious creature under the control of the Red Queen.*

Brillig: *4 o'clock in the afternoon. When one begins broiling things for dinner.*

 Crims: *The central area of Underland. It is here that the Talking Flowers grow.*

Downal wyth Bluddy Behg Hid: *Down with the Red Queen; Underland Underground Resistance slogan.*

Ezel: *High, go higher, go up.*

Fairfarren: *Farewell; may you travel far under fair skies.*

Faldinal: *The day Absolem ordered the Vorpal Sword to be forged.*

 Frabjous Day: *The day Alice slays the Jabberwocky and frees Underland from the oppression of the Red Queen.*

Frumious: *Dirty and smelly.*

Fustilug: *The day after Shatterky when the Red Queen enslaved the free animals in her palace and forced them to act as furniture, ornaments or sports equipment.*

Futterwacken: *The Underlanders' dance of unbridled joy.*

Gallymoggers: *Crazy.*

Gleb: *The day the sky rained fish for no apparent reason.*

Gribling Day: *The day Alice will return to Underland.*

Gummer Slough: *Dangerous swamp of thick viscous mud.*

 Horunvendush Day: *The day the Red Queen took control of Underland.*

Jabberwocky: *A deadly creature employed as the Red Queen's ultimate weapon.*

Jubjub bird: *A bird under the control of the Red Queen.*

Keltikidik: *In celebration of the White Queen; a day when everyone in Underland wore only white, drank only milk and if they had to tell lies, they could only be white ones.*

Klotchyn: *"Heads up" or "pay attention".*

OUTLANDISH IS A STRANGE, old language, full of weird and wonderful words, and it is only spoken in the Outlands. The Underland Underground Resistance adopted Outlandish as the official language for their political group.

Marmoreal: *The location of the White Queen's castle.*

Naught for usal: *It's no use trying.*

Nunz: *Wait or "Don't go; not now".*

Oraculum: *The Calendar of all the days of Underland since the Beginning. Each day has its own title and illustration.*

Orgal: *To the left.*

Outlands: *The untamed land to the west of Witzend.*

Outlandish: *The old language spoken in the Outlands; used by the Underland Underground Resistance as a code in the revolution against the Red Queen.*

Pishalver: *A vile-tasting potion that makes one shrink.*

Queast: *A land to the east, but "not in the least".*

Quillian: *The following day after Alice returns.*

Saganistute: *A wise person of poetry and vision.*

Salazen Grum: *A port city where the Red Queen lives.*

Shatterky: *The day the White Queen was banished to Marmoreal.*

Shunder: *The first morning that the sun rose on Underland.*

Stang: *To the right.*

Slurvish: *Selfish or self-centred.*

Snud: *A region in the south of Underland.*

Tulgey Wood: *Where Alice meets the Jabberwocky.*

Underland: *The real name for the place Alice calls "Wonderland".*

Upelkuchen: *A cake that makes one grow.*

Witzend: *The western land where the Hatter and the Cheshire Cat were born.*

Yadder: *Far away; "Way yadder beyond the Crossling in Snud".*

Zounder: *A warning to "look out behind you"!*

Curious Language

When Alice hears Outlandish being spoken for the first time, she is very confused. The words sound familiar to her but they are not quite right – a bit like Underland.

INDEX

A

armour 40, 61, 64
Ascot, Hamish 13, 14, 15, 67
Ascot, Lady 13, 14, 15, 36, 67
Ascot, Lord 13, 14, 36, 67
Aunt Imogene 12

B

Bandersnatch 24, 32–33, 34, 52, 68
Bandersnatch's eye 25, 32, 33
battle ruins 65
battles 21, 24, 27, 41, 65
Bayard 59
breeches 24, 32
butterfly 28, 67

C

cake 7, 17, 56
Caterpillar (Absolem) 26, 28–29, 30, 31, 34, 63, 64, 67, 68
Chattaway, Faith 14, 15, 67
Chattaway, Fiona 14, 15, 67
Cheshire Cat (Chessur) 11, 48, 52–53, 69
chess 60, 61
China 67
courtier 40
Crims 7, 38, 68
Crimson sea 42
croquet 14, 44–45
crowns 39, 58, 65

D

Dodo 11, 31, 48
Dominion Over Living Things 38
doors 17, 18, 62
Dormouse (Mallymkun) 24–25, 31, 32, 33, 47, 56, 57
dreams 11, 12, 15, 16, 19, 24, 48, 62, 64
dresses 11, 16, 57, 66
"Drink Me" liquid 17

E

"Eat Me" cake 17

F

fish butler 38
flamingos 43, 44, 61
Frabjous Day 31, 34, 64–65, 68
frog footmen 38, 39, 43
furniture 43, 58, 68
Futterwacken 46, 64, 66, 68

G

gardens 17, 36, 63
glass table 17
gloves 11
Griblig Day 31, 68
guillotine 53
Gummer Slough 7, 68

H

hat pins 24, 25, 31, 32, 47, 50
hats 38, 46, 50, 51
heads 27, 38, 39, 40, 41, 42, 44, 45, 47, 50, 51, 58, 60, 61
healing arts 59
hedgehogs 44
Hightopp Clan 30, 34, 39, 46, 50, 52, 63
Horunvendush Day 9, 30, 46, 63, 68

I

Jabberwocky 9, 28, 30, 31, 33, 34–35, 39, 46, 52, 58, 64, 65, 66, 68, 69
jacket 25
Jubjub bird 27, 68

K

Keltikidik 7, 68
key 17, 62
Kingsleigh, Alice 8, 9, 10–11, 12, 13, 14, 15, 16, 17, 20, 21, 22, 23, 24, 25, 26, 28, 30, 31, 32, 33, 35, 38, 40, 41, 46, 52, 56, 57, 59, 62, 64, 65, 66, 67, 68, 69
Kingsleigh, Charles 10, 11, 12, 14, 17, 67
Kingsleigh, Helen 10, 11, 13, 17, 67
Knave of Hearts (Ilosovic Stayne) 38, 39, 40, 41, 57, 65

LONDON, NEW YORK, MELBOURNE,
MUNICH, AND DELHI

Editor Jo Casey
Designer Julie Thompson
Senior Editor Laura Gilbert
Senior Designer Lisa Sodeau
Managing Editor Catherine Saunders
Art Director Lisa Lanzarini
Publishing Manager Simon Beecroft
Category Publisher Alex Allan
Production Editor Clare McLean
Print Production Nick Seston

First published in Great Britain in 2010 by
Dorling Kindersley Limited,
80 Strand, London, WC2R 0RL

Based on the classic story by Lewis Carroll
Based on the screenplay by Linda Woolverton
Produced by Richard D. Zanuck, Joe Roth, Suzanne Todd, and Jennifer Todd
Directed by Tim Burton
Copyright © 2010 Disney Enterprises, Inc.

Page design copyright © 2010 Dorling Kindersley Limited

2 4 6 8 10 9 7 5 3 1
177445—12/09

A CIP catalogue record for this book
is available from the British Library.

ISBN: 978-1-40535-259-8

Reproduced by Alta Images, London
Printed at Tlaciarne BB s.r.o, Slovak Republic

Discover more at
www.dk.com

DK would like to thank:
Dominique Flynn, Al Giuliani,
Lauren Kressel, Chelsea
Nissenbaum, Erik Schmudde,
Rich Thomas and Shiho Tilley
at Disney Publishing.